Words of Comfort
from Holy Scripture

Robert Hellam, editor

Robert Hellam, Publisher
Seaside, California

Dedicated to all past and present members of our weeknight prayer and Bible-study group, now in its twenty-third year.

Hellam, Robert, editor
Words of Comfort from Holy Scripture

Introduction

This is a collection of Bible verses that I have compiled over the years for various purposes, verses that have been comforting to me. This book is offered in the hope that it will also be of comfort to other people.

One purpose, although obviously not the only purpose, of God's holy Word is to comfort His people. Germane to this purpose are these famous words from the prophet

4

Isaiah: "Comfort ye, comfort ye my people,
saith your God. Speak ye comfortably. . . ."

Human Sinfulness and God's Forgiveness

These verses were put together many years ago for our Wednesday-night small group. They speak to the reality presented in the Bible, that human beings are by nature completely sinful and apparently beyond redemption. But the good news is that we are not in fact beyond redemption. We can be redeemed "from the wrath that is to come" (Matthew 3:7) by receiving Jesus Christ as both Savior and Lord.

Perhaps some readers will be interested in the history of our small group. It began back when Connie (my wife) and I were still members of a United Methodist church. Inspired by the example of John Wesley and the early Methodists, I preached a sermon (as a Certified Lay Speaker) one Sunday in which I encouraged our seemingly somnolent church to follow that example. I said, "We should meet during the week for prayer and fellowship and Bible study, not just on Sundays."

To my surprise, one member (Devra Johnson) took me up on my words and challenged me to form such a small group. That was back in early 1992, and all these years later we are still meeting every week, although Connie and I are the only charter members still in the group.

The verses in this section were literally cut and pasted from photocopied pages of the Bible, in the days before personal computers.

THE LORD looked down from heaven upon the children of men, to see if there were any that did understand, and seek God. They are all gone aside, they are altogether become filthy: there is none that doeth good, no, not one.[1]

And Jesus said . . . "None is good, save One, that is, God."[2]

It is of the LORD's mercies that we are not consumed, because His compassions fail not.[3]

The LORD is merciful and gracious, slow to anger, and plenteous in mercy. . . . He hath not dealt with us after our sins; nor rewarded us according to our iniquities. For as the heaven is high above the earth, so great is His mercy. . . . As far as the east is from the west, so far hath He removed our transgressions from us.[4]

---

[1] Psalm 14:2-3 (all verses from the King James Version, unless otherwise noted)
[2] Luke 18:19
[3] Lamentations 3:22
[4] Psalm 103:8-12

He that covereth his sins shall not prosper: but whoso confesseth and forsaketh them shall have mercy.[5]

Confess your faults one to another, and pray one for another, that ye may be healed.[6]

If we confess our sins, He is faithful and just to forgive us our sins, and to cleanse us from all unrighteousness.[7]

. . . Do not call anything impure that God has made clean.[8]

[God the Father] hath delivered us from the power of darkness, and hath translated us into the Kingdom of His dear Son.[9]

For by grace are ye saved through faith; and that not of yourselves: it is the gift of God: not of works, lest any man should boast.[10]

---

[5] Proverbs 28:13

[6] James 5:16

[7] I John 1:9

[8] Acts 10:15, New International Version (NIV)

[9] Colossians 1:13

[10] Ephesians 2:8-9

Therefore being justified by faith, we have peace with God through our Lord Jesus Christ.[11]

For sin shall not have dominion over you: for ye are not under the Law, but under grace.[12]

[Be] confident of this very thing, that He which hath begun a good work in you will perform it until the Day of Jesus Christ.[13]

For God's gift and His call are irrevocable.[14]

If the Son therefore shall make you free, ye shall be free indeed.[15]

Stand fast therefore in the liberty wherewith Christ hath made us free, and be not entangled again with the yoke of bondage.[16]

For God sent not His Son into the world to condemn the world; but that the world through Him might be saved.[17]

---

[11] Romans 5:1
[12] Romans 6:14
[13] Philippians 1:6
[14] Romans 11:29, NIV
[15] John 8:36
[16] Galatians 5:1
[17] John 3:17

There is therefore now no condemnation to them which are in Christ Jesus. . . .[18]

[Cast] all your care upon Him; for He careth for you.[19]

And let the peace of God rule in your hearts. . . .[20]

Submit yourselves therefore to God. Resist the devil, and he will flee from you.[21]

Rejoice not against me, O mine enemy: when I fall, I shall arise; when I sit in darkness, the LORD shall be a light unto me.[22]

When I said, "My foot slippeth"; Thy mercy, O LORD, held me up.[23]

I do not understand what I do. For what I want to do I do not do, but what I hate I do.[24]

---

[18] Romans 8:1
[19] I Peter 5:7
[20] Colossians 3:15
[21] James 4:7
[22] Micah 7:8
[23] Psalm 94:18
[24] Romans 7:15, NIV

And He said unto me, "My grace is sufficient for thee: for My strength is made perfect in weakness."[25]

Then came Peter to Him, and said, "Lord, how oft shall my brother sin against me, and I forgive him? till seven times?" Jesus saith unto him, "I say not unto thee, 'Until seven times': but, 'Until seventy times seven.' "[26]
Since your Father in heaven is perfect, you are to be perfect.[27]
And forgive us our sins; for we also forgive everyone that is indebted to us. And lead us not into temptation; but deliver us from evil.[28]

Humble yourselves in the sight of the Lord, and He shall lift you up.[29]
He will turn again, He will have compassion upon us; He will subdue our iniquities; and

---

[25] II Corinthians 12:9
[26] Matthew 18:21-22
[27] Matthew 5:48, *The Greatest Story*
[28] Luke 11:4
[29] James 4:10

Thou wilt cast all their sins into the depths of the sea.[30]

I, even I, am He that blotteth out thy transgressions for Mine own sake, and I will not remember thy sins.[31]

For with God nothing shall be impossible.[32]

. . . Be strong and of a good courage; be not afraid, neither be thou dismayed: for the LORD thy God is with thee whithersoever thou goest.[33]

---

[30] Micah 7:19
[31] Isaiah 43:25
[32] Luke 1:37
[33] Joshua 1:9

14

My Own Favorite Verse

(Clearly, this verse contains words of comfort from Jesus that can also be taken as words of caution.)

And, lo, I Am with you always, even unto the end of the world.   Amen (Matthew 28:20b).

16

My Favorite Passage

In [Christ Jesus] also are ye circumcised with the circumcision made without hands, in putting off the body of the sins of the flesh by the circumcision of Christ: buried with him in baptism, wherein also ye are risen with him through the faith of the operation of God, who hath raised him from the dead. And you, being dead in your sins and the uncircumcision of your flesh, hath he quickened together with him, having forgiven you all trespasses; blotting out the handwriting of ordinances that was against us, which was contrary to us, and took it out of the way, nailing it to his cross; and having spoiled principalities and powers, he made a show of them openly, triumphing over them in it (Colossians 2:11-15).

My Favorite Old Testament Book

Psalms

My Favorite New Testament Book

The Gospel of John

(Use the space below and on the next page to write down your favorites.)

20

Apologetics

The next three sections of this book are really some tools for what is called "apologetics." Our modern use of the words *apology* and *apologetic* may mislead us in this area, but the original meaning of the word *apology* was not to say, "I was wrong, and I am sorry." On the contrary, the word designated a statement from a person to explain why that person's beliefs or actions were right.

Christian apologetics does not necessarily seek to "prove" the truth of our faith, but it does show that it is not illogical, not absurd, not a blind leap into the unknown, for a person to have Christian faith.

If you are interested in the literature of Christian apologetics, there are a number of good works out there. Some of Hank Hanegraaff's books, for example, contain such good tools as his acronym *MAPS*, defending the truth of the Bible by pointing out the good evidence for its truth: there is better *manuscript* evidence than exists for many other ancient documents; *archeology* has often upheld, and never disproved, Biblical reports; *predictive prophecy* in the Bible has been uniformly accurate; and *statistical probability* militates in favor of Biblical reliability.

Classics in the field of apologetics are such works as *Mere Christianity* by C. S. Lewis, *Evidence That Demands a Verdict* by Josh McDowell, *The Case for Christ* by Lee Strobel, *Basic Christianity* by John R. W. Stott, and *Reason to Believe* by R. C. Sproul. Also worthwhile are such works as *Faith*

Founded on Fact by John Warwick Montgomery; *Pensées* by Blaise Pascal; *Jesus 2000* by George Carey; *Intellectuals Don't Need God, and Other Modern Myths* by Alister McGrath; *Know the Truth* by Bruce Milne; *What Christians Believe* by Johnson and Webber; *Simply Christian* by N. T. Wright; *Know What You* Believe by Paul E. Little; *What Christianity Is All About* by Alan Scholes; *So What's the Difference?* by Fritz Ridenour; and several others.

"The Romans Road"

"The Romans Road" is a favorite evangelism tool for many believers to use in their witnessing to people who are not yet believers—or, as some prefer to say, people who are still "pre-Christians." If you guide a person through these verses from Romans, you have made a good statement of what the Gospel is all about.

For all have sinned, and come short of the glory of God (Romans 3:23).

For the wages of sin is death; but the gift of God is eternal life through Jesus Christ our Lord (6:23).

But God commendeth his love toward us, in that, while we were yet sinners, Christ died for us (5:8).

. . . If thou shalt confess with thy mouth the Lord Jesus, and shalt believe in thine heart that God hath raised him from the dead, thou shalt be saved. For with the heart man believeth unto righteousness, and with the mouth confession is made unto salvation (10:9-10).

I beseech you therefore, brethren, by the mercies of God, that ye present your bodies a living sacrifice, holy, acceptable unto God, which is your reasonable service. And be not conformed to this world: but be ye transformed by the renewing of your mind, that ye may prove what is that good, and acceptable, and perfect, will of God (12:1-2).

28

Authority of Christ
The Only Way

I was once speaking to an ordained minister from another denomination. She claimed that the only place where the Bible says that Jesus is the only Way to the Father is in the Gospel of John. And according to her, the Gospel of John is not authoritative anyway. Of course, I believe she was wrong on both counts. Here are some verses from different places in the New Testament that make that point.

30

[*Jesus says*] All things are delivered unto me of my Father: and no man knoweth the Son, but the Father; neither knoweth any man the Father, save the Son, and he to whomsoever the Son will reveal him (Matthew 11:27).

[*Jesus says*] Whosoever therefore shall be ashamed of me and of my words in this adulterous and sinful generation; of him also shall the Son of man be ashamed, when he cometh in the glory of his Father with the holy angels (Mark 8:38).

[*Jesus says*] All things are delivered to me of my Father: and no man knoweth who the Son is, but the Father; and who the Father is, but the Son, and he to whom the Son will reveal him (Luke 10:22).

[*Jesus says*] Also I say unto you, Whosoever shall confess me before men, him shall the Son of man also confess before the angels of God: but he that denieth me before men shall be denied before the angels of God (12:8-9).

Jesus said unto him, "I Am the way, the truth, and the life; no man cometh unto the Father, but by me" (John 14:6).

Be it known unto you all, and to all the people of Israel, that by the name of Jesus Christ of Nazareth, whom ye crucified, whom God raised from the dead, even by him doth this man stand here before you whole. This is the stone which was set at nought of you builders, which is become the head of the corner. Neither is there salvation in any other: for there is none other name under heaven given among men, whereby we must be saved (Acts 4:10-12).

Authority of Scripture

The Bible testifies several times and in many different ways about its own authority. If you ever have doubts, these verses might help put them to rest.

Ye shall not add unto the word which I command you, neither shall ye diminish ought from it, that ye may keep the commandments of the LORD your God which I command you (Deuteronomy 4:2).

What thing soever I command you, observe to do it: thou shalt not add thereto, nor diminish from it (12:32).

And the LORD thy God will make thee plenteous in every work of thine hand, in the fruit of thy body, and in the fruit of thy cattle, and in the fruit of thy land, for good: for the LORD will again rejoice over thee for good, as he rejoiced over thy fathers: if thou shalt hearken unto the voice of the LORD thy God, to keep his commandments and his statutes which are written in this book of the law, and if thou turn unto the LORD thy God with all thine heart, and with all thy soul (30:9-10).

The grass withereth, the flower fadeth: but the word of our God shall stand forever (Isaiah 40:8).

[*Jesus says*] Think not that I am come to destroy the law, or the prophets: I am not come to destroy, but to fulfill. For verily I say unto you, Till heaven and earth pass, one jot or one tittle shall in no wise pass from the law, till all be fulfilled. Whosoever therefore shall break one of these least commandments, and shall teach men so, he shall be called the least in the kingdom of heaven: but whosoever shall do and teach them, the same shall be called great in the kingdom of heaven (Matthew 5:17-19).

[*Jesus says*] Heaven and earth shall pass away, but my words shall not pass away (24:35).

And Jesus answered him, saying, "It is written that man shall not live by bread alone, but by every word of God" (Luke 4:4).

And [Jesus] came to Nazareth, where he had been brought up: and, as his custom was, he went into the synagogue on the Sabbath day, and stood up for to read. And there was delivered unto him the book of the prophet Isaiah. And when he had opened the book, he found the place where it was written, "The Spirit of the Lord is upon me, because he hath anointed me to preach the gospel to the poor; he hath sent me to heal the brokenhearted, to preach deliverance to the captives, and recovering of sight to the blind, to set at liberty them that are bruised, to preach the acceptable year of the Lord." And he closed the book, and he gave it again to the minister, and sat down. And the eyes of all them that were in the synagogue were fastened on him. And he began to say unto them, "This day is this scripture fulfilled in your ears" (4:16-21).

Then [Jesus] said unto them, "O fools, and slow of heart to believe all that the prophets have spoken: ought not Christ to have suffered these things, and to enter into his glory?" And beginning at Moses and all the prophets, he expounded unto them in all the scriptures the things concerning himself (24:25-27).

And [Jesus] said unto them, "These are the words which I spoke unto you, while I was yet with you, that all things must be fulfilled, which were written in the law of Moses, and in the prophets, and in the psalms, concerning me." Then opened he their understanding, that they might understand the scriptures, and said unto them, "Thus it is written, and thus it behooved Christ to suffer, and to rise from the dead the third day: and that repentance and remission of sins should be preached in his name among all nations, beginning at Jerusalem" (24:44-47).

And [Jesus'] disciples remembered that it was written, "The zeal of thine house hath eaten me up." Then answered the Jews and said unto him, "What sign showest thou unto us, seeing that thou doest these things?" Jesus answered and said unto them, "Destroy this temple, and in three days I will raise it up." Then said the Jews, "Forty and six years was this temple in building, and wilt thou rear it up in three days?" But he spoke of the temple of his body. When therefore he was risen from the dead, his disciples remembered that he had said this unto them; and they believed the scripture, and the word which Jesus had said (John 2:17-22).

[*Jesus says*] Do not think that I will accuse you to the Father: there is one that accuseth you, even Moses, in whom ye trust. For had ye believed Moses, ye would have believed me: for he wrote of me. But if you believe not his writings, how shall ye believe my words? (5:45-57).

[*Jesus says*] . . . The scripture cannot be broken . . . (10:35).

And the brethren immediately sent away Paul and Silas by night unto Berea: who coming thither went into the synagogue of the Jews. These were more noble than those in Thessalonica, in that they received the word with all readiness of mind, and searched the scriptures daily, whether those things were so. Therefore many of them believed; also of honorable women which were Greeks, and of men, not a few (Acts 17:10-12).

And when they agreed not among themselves, they departed, after that Paul had spoken one word, "Well spoke the Holy Ghost by Isaiah the prophet unto our fathers ..." (28:25).

What advantage then hath the Jew? or what profit is there of circumcision? Much every way: chiefly, because that unto them were committed the oracles of God (Romans 3:1-2).

For whatsoever things were written aforetime were written for our learning, that we through patience and comfort of the scriptures might have hope (15:4).

But I certify you, brethren, that the gospel which was preached of me is not after man, for I neither received it of man, neither was I taught it, but by the revelation of Jesus Christ (Galatians 1:11-12).

In [Jesus] ye also trusted, after that ye heard the word of truth, the gospel of your salvation: in whom also after that ye believed, ye were sealed with that holy Spirit of promise (Ephesians 1:13).

Let the elders that rule well be counted worthy of double honor, especially they who labor in the word and doctrine. For the scripture saith, "Thou shalt not muzzle the ox that treadeth out the corn." And, "The laborer is worthy of his reward" (I Timothy 5:17-18).

[*The above passage is significant especially because Paul here identifies both the words of Moses in the Old Testament, and the words of Jesus that would be recorded in the New Testament, as "scripture."*]

But continue thou in the things which thou hast learned and hast been assured of, knowing of whom thou hast learned them; and that from a child thou hast known the holy scriptures, which are able to make thee wise unto salvation through faith which is in Christ Jesus. All scripture is given by inspiration of God, and is profitable for doctrine, for reproof, for correction, for instruction in righteousness: that the man of God may be perfect, thoroughly furnished unto all good works (II Timothy 3:14-17).

Wherefore (as the Holy Ghost saith) "Today if ye will hear his voice . . ." (Hebrews 3:7).

[*The significance of the above verse is that it clearly identifies the words of the Old Testament as really the words of the Holy Spirit.*]

For the word of God is quick and powerful, and sharper than any two-edged sword, piercing even to the dividing asunder of soul and spirit, and of the joints and marrow, and is a discerner of the thoughts and intents of the heart (4:12).

Of which salvation the prophets have inquired and searched diligently, who prophesied of the grace that should come unto you: searching what, or what manner of time the Spirit of Christ which was in them did signify, when [he] testified beforehand the suffering of Christ, and the glory that should follow, unto whom it was revealed, that not unto themselves, but unto us they did minister the things, which are now reported unto you by them that have preached the gospel unto you with the Holy Ghost sent down from heaven: which things the angels desire to look into (I Peter 1:10-12).

For the prophecy came not in old time by the will of man: but holy men of God spoke as they were moved by the Holy Ghost (II Peter 1:21).

And account that the longsuffering of our Lord is salvation; even as our beloved brother Paul also according to the wisdom given unto him hath written unto you; as also in all his epistles, speaking in them of these things; in which are some things hard to be understood, which they that are unlearned and unstable wrest, as they do also the other scriptures, unto their own destruction (3:15-16).

[*The above passage is quoted to show that even during the lifetime of Paul his letters were already recognized as Scripture.*]

For I testify unto every man that heareth the words of the prophecy of this book, If any man shall add unto these things, God shall add unto him the plagues that are written in this book: and if any man shall take away from the words of the book of this prophecy, God shall take away his part out of the book of life, and out of the holy city, and from the things which are written in this book. He which testifieth these things saith, "Surely I come quickly." Amen. Even so, come, Lord Jesus (Revelation 22:18-20).

God's Will for Humankind

I have sometimes been dismayed to hear some people advance a view of God that seems to me somewhat blasphemous. That view is that God, before the beginning of time, planned to create some human beings for the pleasant purpose of consigning them to hell, so that they would never have a chance at eternal life. Although I consider myself to be a Calvinist, I think such a view depicts God as a hateful monster.

In my opinion, there is an element of mystery in our election, since it involves apparently contradictory truths that we must hold in tension. We know that we do nothing to earn our own salvation, and that God chooses to save us out of His compassion, in spite of our many imperfections, once we have repented of our sins and believed in the Lord Jesus Christ. At that moment when we first believed, many of us had the clear sensation that we were making a choice, and that our choice made an eternal difference in our lives. And yet we still understand that

God chose us, and that it was His choice that made the difference.

In human terms, this may seem paradoxical, but I believe that the reality of God's choice of us and of our actively placing our trust in Jesus are reconciled in the mind of God. That's good enough for me, and I find comfort in the following Bible verses that display God's love and His goodwill toward His creation.

For I know the thoughts that I think toward you, saith the LORD, thoughts of peace, and not of evil, to give you an expected end (Jeremiah 29:11).

[*Some will object that the promise above is solely to Israel and not to the Church, but since Israel finds its fulfillment in Jesus and in His Church, I am certain that we Christians can also claim that promise.*]

[*Jesus says*] Even so it is not the will of your Father which is in heaven, that one of these little ones should perish (Matthew 18:14).

[*Jesus says*] For God sent not his Son into the world to condemn the world, but that the world through him might be saved (John 3:17).

For this is good and acceptable in the sight of God our Savior, who will have all men to be saved, and to come unto the knowledge of the truth (I Timothy 2:3-4).

The Lord is not slack concerning his promise, as some men count slackness, but is longsuffering to us-ward, not willing that any should perish, but that all should come to repentance (II Peter 3:9).

52

The Old in the New

Do you recognize, in these Old Testament verses, the most famous prayer in the New Testament?

Have we not all one Father? hath not one God created us? . . .[34]

Look down from Thy holy habitation, from heaven, and bless Thy people. . . .[35]

Bless the LORD, O my soul; and all that is within me, bless His holy Name.[36]

---

[34] Malachi 2:10
[35] Deuteronomy 26:15
[36] Psalm 103:1

[His] Kingdom is an everlasting Kingdom, and all dominions shall serve and obey Him.[37]

Teach me to do Thy will; for Thou art my God. . . .[38]

. . . Give me neither poverty nor riches, but give me only my daily bread.[39]

. . . Deliver us and forgive our sins for Your Name's sake.[40]

. . . Forgive, I pray thee now, the trespass of thy brethren, and their sin. . . .[41]

---

[37] Daniel 7:27
[38] Psalm 143:10
[39] Proverbs 30:8, NIV
[40] Psalm 79:9, NIV
[41] Genesis 50:17

And the LORD said unto Satan, ". . . Upon [the man] himself put not forth thine hand."[42]

Thine, O LORD, is the greatness, and the power, and the glory, and the victory and the majesty: for all that is in the heaven and in the earth is Thine; Thine is the Kingdom, O LORD, and Thou art exalted as Head above all.[43]

---

[42] Job 1:12
[43] I Chronicles 29:11

56

A Nice Coincidence
of Biblical Place Names and English Words

"Thus saith the LORD God . . . I will pour My fury upon Sin . . . and I will cut off the multitude of No" (Ezekiel 30:13-15).

58

Books by Robert Hellam

*Sonnets of David, Book I: A Poetic
        Paraphrase of Psalms 1-41*
        (Lincoln: Writers Club Press,
        2000).

*Sonnets of David, Books II-III: A Poetic
        Paraphrase of Psalms 42-89*
        (Lincoln: Writers Club Press, 2001).

*Sonnets of David, Books IV-V: A Poetic
        Paraphrase of Psalms 90-150*
        (Lincoln: iUniverse, 2003).

Witnesses of the Nativity: Poems (San
        Francisco: Blurb.com, 2007).

*"Some New Thing": Paul and the
        Philosophers: Paul's Epistemology
        and the Postmodern Impasse*
        (Charleston: CreateSpace, 2011).

The Congregational Minute (Charleston:
        CreateSpace,   2012).

Selected Poems 1964-1992 (Charleston: CreateSpace, 2012).

Leadership: Basic Principles from the Book of Proverbs (Charleston: CreateSpace, 2013).

Across the Centuries: Poems 1992-2006 (Charleston: CreateSpace, 2013).

Huckleberries in the Fog: Poems 2006-2014 (Charleston: CreateSpace, 2014).

(All the books listed above are available either from the publisher or from Amazon.com, with the exception of *Witnesses of the Nativity*, which is available only from the publisher.)

69907771R00035

Made in the USA
San Bernardino, CA
23 February 2018